Knit Cardigan

Perfect Ways to Update Your Wardrobe

DEDICATION

Contents

V-neck Cardigan

(Shown in Child Size only)

MATERIALS

Sizes XS/S M L XL 2/3XL 4/5XL

Caron® Simply Soft® (Heathers: 5 oz/141.7 g; 250 yds/228 m): 4 5 5 6 7 8 balls

Caron® Simply Soft® (Solids: 6 oz/170.1 g; 315 yds/288 m): 4 4 5 5 6 7 balls

Sizes U.S. 7 (4.5 mm) and U.S. 8 (5 mm) knitting needles or size needed to obtain gauge. 3 st holders. 5 buttons.

SIZES

To fit bust/chest measurement

Extra-Small/Small: 28-34" [71-86.5 cm]

Medium: 36-38" [91.5-96.5 cm]

Large: 40-42" [101.5-106.5 cm]

Extra-Large: 44-46" [112-117 cm]

2/3 X-Large: 48-54" [122-137 cm]

4/5 X-Large: 56-62" [142-157.5 cm]

Finished bust/chest

Extra-Small/Small 37" [94 cm]

Medium 40½" [103 cm]

Large 44½" [113 cm]

Extra-Large 49" [124.5 cm]

2/3 X-Large 55" [140 cm]

4/5 X-Large 63" [160 cm]

ABBREVIATIONS

Beg = Beginning

Cont = Continue(ity)

Dec = Decrease(ing)

Inc = Increase(ing)

K = Knit

K2tog = Knit next 2 stitches together

P = Purl

P2tog = Purl next 2 stitches together

P2togtbl = Purl next 2 stitches together through back loops

Rem = Remaining

Rep = Repeat

RS = Right side

Ssk = Slip next 2 stitches knitwise one at a time. Pass them back onto left-hand needle, then knit through back loops together

St(s) = Stitch(es)

GAUGE: 18 sts and 24 rows = 4" [10 cm] in stocking st with larger needles.

INSTRUCTIONS

The instructions are written for smallest size. If changes are necessary for larger sizes the instructions will be written thus ( ). When only one number is given in, it applies to all sizes.

BACK

With smaller needles cast on 82 (90-98-110-122-138) sts.

1st row: (RS). *K2. P2. Rep from * to last 2 sts. K2.

2nd row: *P2. K2. Rep from * to last 2 sts. P2.

Rep last 2 rows (K2. P2) ribbing for 2½" [6 cm], ending on a 2nd row and inc 3 (3-3-1-3-5) st(s) evenly across last row. 85 (93-101-111-125-143) sts.

Change to larger needles and proceed in stocking st until work from beg measures 16 (16-16-16½-16½-16½)" [40.5 (40.5-40.5-42-42-42) cm] for Her Version or 17 (17-17-17½-17½-17½)" [43 (43-43-44.5-44.5-44.5) cm] for His Version, ending on a purl row.

Shape raglans: Cast off 2 (2-3-3-4-4) sts at beg of next 2 rows. 81 (89-95-105-117-135) sts.

Sizes 2/3XL and 4/5XL only:

1st row: (RS). K2. ssk. Knit to last 4 sts. K2tog. K2.

2nd row: P2. P2tog. Purl to last 4 sts. P2togtbl. P2.

Rep last 2 rows (4-14) times more, then 1st row once. (95-73) sts.

Purl 1 row.

Sizes M, L, XL, 2/3XL and 4/5XL only:

1st row: (RS). K2. ssk. Knit to last 4 sts. K2tog. K2.

2nd row: P2. P2tog. Purl to last 4 sts. P2togtbl. P2.

3rd row: As 1st row.

4th row: Purl.

Rep last 4 rows (1-1-5-3-2) time(s) more. (77-83-69-71-55) sts.

All sizes: 1st row: (RS). K2. ssk. Knit to last 4 sts. K2tog. K2.

2nd row: Purl.

Rep last 2 rows 23 (21-23-16-16-8) times more. 33 (33-35-35-37-37) sts. Cast off.

LEFT FRONT

With smaller needles cast on 43(47-51-55-63-71) sts.

1st row: (RS). *K2. P2. Rep from * to last 3 sts. K3.

2nd row: K1. *P2. K2. Rep from * to last 2 sts. P2.

Rep last 2 rows (K2. P2) ribbing for 2½" [6 cm], ending on a 2nd row and inc 0 (0-0-1-0-1) st(s) in center of last row. 43 (47-51-56-63-72) sts.

Change to larger needles and proceed in stocking st until work from beg measures 16 (16-16-16½-16½-16½)" [40.5 (40.5-40.5-42-42-42) cm] for Her Version or 17 (17-17-17½-17½-17½)" [43 (43-43-44.5-44.5-44.5) cm] for His Version, ending on a purl row.

Shape raglan: Cast off 2 (2-3-3-4-4) sts at beg of next row. 41 (45-48-53-59-68) sts. Purl 1 row.

Size XS/S only: Shape neck:

1st row: (RS). K2. ssk. Knit to last 2 sts. K2tog.

2nd row: Purl.

Rep last 2 rows 6 times more. 27 sts rem.

1st row: (RS). K2. ssk. Knit to end of row.

2nd row: Purl.

3rd row: K2. ssk. Knit to last 2 sts. K2tog.

4th row: Purl.

Rep last 4 rows 6 times more. 6 sts rem.

Next row: (RS). K2. ssk. K2tog.

Next row: P4.

Next row: K2. ssk.

Next row: P3.

Next row: K3tog. Fasten off.

Sizes M, L and XL only:

1st row: (RS). K2. ssk. Knit to end of row.

2nd row: Purl to last 4 sts. P2togtbl. P2.

Shape neck: 1st row: (RS). K2. ssk. Knit to last 2 sts. K2tog.

2nd row: Purl.

3rd row: As 1st row.

4th row: Purl to last 4 sts. P2togtbl. P2.

Rep last 4 rows (0-0-1) time(s) more. (38-41-41) sts rem.

Sizes M and L only:

1st row: (RS). K2. ssk. Knit to last 2 sts. K2tog.

2nd row: Purl.

Rep last 2 rows 3 times more. (30-33) sts rem.

1st row: (RS). K2. ssk. Knit to end of row.

2nd row: Purl.

3rd row: K2. ssk. Knit to last 2 sts. K2tog.

4th row: Purl.

Rep last 4 rows (7-8) times more. 6 sts rem.

Next row: (RS). K2. ssk. K2tog.

Next row: P4.

Next row: K2. ssk.

Next row: P3.

Next row: K3tog. Fasten off.

Size XL only:

1st row: (RS). K2. ssk. Knit to last 2 sts. K2tog.

2nd row: Purl.

3rd row: K2. ssk. Knit to end of row.

4th row: Purl to last 4 sts. P2togtbl. P2.

Rep last 4 rows twice more. 29 sts rem.

1st row: (RS). K2. ssk. Knit to last 2 sts. K2tog.

2nd row: Purl.

3rd row: K2. ssk. Knit to end of row.

4th row: Purl.

Rep last 4 rows 7 times more. 5 sts rem.

Next row: (RS). K2. ssk. K1.

Next row: P4.

Next row: K2. ssk.

Next row: P3.

Next row: K3tog. Fasten off.

Sizes 2/3XL and 4/5XL only:

1st row: (RS). K2. ssk. Knit to end of row.

2nd row: Purl to last 4 sts. P2togtbl. P2.

Rep last 2 rows 3 times more. (51-60) sts.

Size 4/5XL only: Shape neck:

1st row: (RS). K2. ssk. Knit to last 2 sts. K2tog.

2nd row: Purl to last 4 sts. P2togtbl. P2.

Rep last 2 rows 8 times more. 33 sts.

1st row: (RS). K2. ssk. Knit to end of row.

2nd row: Purl.

3rd row: K2. ssk. Knit to last 2 sts. K2tog.

4th row: Purl to last 4 sts. P2togtbl. P2.

Rep last 4 rows 3 times more. 17 sts.

1st row: (RS). K2. ssk. Knit to end of row.

2nd row: Purl.

3rd row: K2. ssk. Knit to last 2 sts. K2tog.

4th row: Purl.

Rep last 4 rows 3 times more. 5 sts rem.

Next row: (RS). K2. ssk. K1.

Next row: P4.

Next row: K2. ssk.

Next row: P3.

Next row: K3tog. Fasten off.

Size 2/3XL only: Shape neck:

1st row: (RS). K2. ssk. Knit to last 2 sts. K2tog.

2nd row: Purl to last 4 sts. P2togtbl. P2.

3rd row: As 1st row.

4th row: Purl.

Rep last 4 rows 3 times more. 31 sts rem.

1st row: (RS). K2. ssk. Knit to last 2 sts. K2tog.

2nd row: Purl to last 4 sts. P2togtbl. P2.

3rd row: K2. ssk. Knit to end of row.

4th row: Purl.

5th row: As 1st row.

6th row: Purl.

7th row: As 3rd row.

8th row: Purl.

Rep 5th to 8th rows 7 times more. 3 sts rem.

Next row: ssk. K1.

Next row: P2.

Next row: K2tog. Fasten off.

RIGHT FRONT

With smaller needles cast on 43 (47-51-55-63-71) sts.

1st row: (RS). K3. *P2. K2. Rep from * to end of row.

2nd row: *P2. K2. Rep from * to last 3 sts. P2. K1.

Rep last 2 rows (K2. P2) ribbing for 2½" [6 cm], ending on a 2nd row and inc 0 (0-0-1-0-1) st(s) in center of last row. 43 (47-51-56-63-72) sts.

Change to larger needles and proceed in stocking st until work from beg measures 16 (16-16-16½-16½-16½)" [40.5 (40.5-40.5-42-42-42) cm] for Her Version or 17 (17-17-17½-17½-17½)" [43 (43-43-44.5-44.5-44.5) cm] for His Version, ending on a knit row.

Shape raglan: Cast off 2 (2-3-3-4-4) sts at beg of next row. 41 (45-48-53-59-68) sts.

Size XS/S only: Shape neck:

1st row: (RS). ssk. Knit to last 4 sts. K2tog. K2.

2nd row: Purl.

Rep last 2 rows 6 times more. 27 sts rem.

1st row: (RS). Knit to last 4 sts. K2tog. K2.

2nd row: Purl.

3rd row: ssk. Knit to last 4 sts. K2tog. K2.

4th row: Purl.

Rep last 4 rows 6 times more. 6 sts rem.

Next row: (RS). ssk. K2tog. K2.

Next row: P4.

Next row: ssk. K2.

Next row: P3.

13

Next row: K3tog. Fasten off.

Sizes M, L and XL only:

1st row: (RS). Knit to last 4 sts. K2tog. K2.

2nd row: P2. P2tog. Purl to end of row.

Shape neck: 1st row: (RS). ssk. Knit to last 4 sts. K2tog. K2.

2nd row: Purl.

3rd row: As 1st row.

4th row: P2. P2tog. Purl to end of row.

Rep last 4 rows (0-0-1) time(s) more. (38-41-41) sts rem.

Sizes M and L only:

1st row: (RS). ssk. Knit to last 4 sts. K2tog. K2.

2nd row: Purl.

Rep last 2 rows 3 times more. (30-33) sts rem.

1st row: (RS). Knit to last 4 sts. K2tog. K2.

2nd row: Purl.

3rd row: ssk. Knit to last 4 sts. K2tog. K2.

4th row: Purl.

Rep last 4 rows (7-8) times more. 6 sts rem.

Next row: (RS). ssk. K2tog. K2.

Next row: P4.

Next row: ssk. K2.

Next row: P3.

Next row: K3tog. Fasten off.

Size XL only:

1st row: (RS). ssk. Knit to last 4 sts. K2tog. K2.

2nd row: Purl.

3rd row: Knit to last 4 sts. K2tog. K2.

4th row: P2. P2tog. Purl to end of row.

Rep last 4 rows twice more. 29 sts rem.

1st row: (RS). ssk. Knit to last 4 sts. K2tog. K2.

2nd row: Purl.

3rd row: Knit to last 4 sts. K2tog. K2.

4th row: Purl.

Rep last 4 rows 7 times more. 5 sts rem.

Next row: (RS). K1. K2tog. K2.

Next row: P4.

Next row: K2tog. K2.

Next row: P3.

Next row: K3tog. Fasten off.

Sizes 2/3XL and 4/5XL only:

1st row: (RS). Knit to last 4 sts. K2tog. K2.

2nd row: P2. P2tog. Purl to end of row.

Rep last 2 rows 3 times more. (51-60) sts.

Size 4/5XL only: Shape neck:

1st row: (RS). ssk. Knit to last 4 sts. K2tog. K2.

2nd row: P2. P2tog. Purl to end of row.

Rep last 2 rows 8 times more. 33 sts.

1st row: (RS). Knit to last 4 sts. K2tog. K2.

2nd row: Purl.

3rd row: ssk. Knit to last 4 sts. K2tog. K2.

4th row: P2. P2tog. Purl to end of row.

Rep last 4 rows 3 times more. 17 sts.

1st row: (RS). Knit to last 4 sts. K2tog. K2.

2nd row: Purl.

3rd row: ssk. Knit to last 4 sts. K2tog. K2.

4th row: Purl.

Rep last 4 rows 3 times more. 5 sts rem.

Next row: (RS). K1. K2tog. K2.

Next row: P4.

Next row: K1. K2tog. K1.

Next row: P3.

Next row: K3tog. Fasten off.

Size 2/3XL only: Shape neck:

1st row: (RS). ssk. Knit to last 4 sts. K2tog. K2.

2nd row: P2. P2tog. Purl to end of row.

3rd row: As 1st row.

4th row: Purl.

Rep last 4 rows 3 times more. 31 sts rem.

1st row: (RS). ssk. Knit to last 4 sts. K2tog. K2.

2nd row: P2. P2tog. Purl to end of row.

3rd row: Knit to last 4 sts. K2tog. K2.

4th row: Purl.

5th row: As 1st row.

6th row: Purl.

7th row: As 3rd row.

8th row: Purl.

Rep 5th to 8th rows 7 times more. 3 sts rem.

Next row: K1. K2tog.

Next row: P2.

Next row: K2tog. Fasten off.

SLEEVES

With smaller needles, cast on 38 (38-42-42-46-46) sts.

Work 2½" [6 cm] in (K2. P2) ribbing as given for Back, ending on a 2nd row and inc 3 sts evenly across last row. 41 (41-45-45-49-49) sts.

Change to larger needles and work 6 rows in stocking st.

Her Sizes only. Inc 1 st each end of next row and following 6th (4th4th-4th-4th-4th-4th) rows until there are 67 (59-63-81-83-85) sts.

Sizes M and L only: Inc 1 st each end of next row and following 6th rows until there are (73-77) sts.

All sizes: Cont even until work from beg measures 17 (17½-17½-16½-16-16)" [43 (44.5-44.5-42-40.5-40.5) cm], ending on a purl row.

His Sizes only: Inc 1 st each end of next row and following 6th (4th4th-4th-4th-4th-4th) rows until there are 59 (55-59-71-69-79) sts, then on following 8th (6th-6th-6th-6th-6th) rows until there are 67 (73-77-81-83-85) sts.

Cont even until work from beg measures 18 (18½-18½-17½-17-17)" [45.5 (47-47-45.5-43-43) cm], ending on a purl row.

All sizes: Shape raglans: Cast off 2 (2-3-3-4-4) sts at beg of next 2 rows. 63 (69-71-75-75-77) sts.

1st row: (RS). K2. ssk. Knit to last 4 sts. K2tog. K2.

2nd row: P2. P2tog. Purl to last 4 sts. P2togtbl. P2.

3rd row: As 1st row.

4th row: Purl.

Rep last 4 rows 2(3-2-2-0-1) time(s) more. 45 (45-53-57-69-65) sts.

1st row: (RS). K2. ssk. Knit to last 4 sts. K2tog. K2.

2nd row: Purl.

Rep last 2 rows 17 (17-21-22-28-26) times more. Leave rem 9 (9-9-11-11-11) sts. Cast off.

FINISHING

Sew raglan seams. Sew side and sleeve seams.

Button and Buttonhole Band:

With smaller needles cast on 9 sts.

1st row: (RS). K2. (P1. K1) 3 times. K1.

2nd row: K1. (P1. K1) 4 times.

Rep last 2 rows until Band, when slightly stretched, measures length to fit up Left Front for Her or Right Front for Him, sewing in place as you knit. Place markers on band for 5 buttons, having bottom button ½" [1 cm] above cast on edge, top button ½" [1 cm] below first front dec and rem 3 buttons spaced evenly between. Cont in ribbing to fit up neck edge, across back neck edge and down opposite neck edge to first button marker.

Make buttonholes as follows:

His Version: 1st row: (RS). Rib 4. Cast off 2 sts. Rib to end of row.

Her Version: 1st row: (RS). Rib 3. Cast off 2 sts. Rib to end of row.

Both Versions: 2nd row: Rib, casting on 2 sts over cast off sts. Cont in ribbing to end of Right Front for Her or Left Front for Him. Cast off in ribbing. Sew on buttons to correspond to buttonholes.

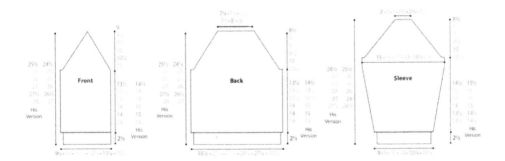

Patchwork Cardigan

MATERIALS

Caron® Big Donut O'Go® (9.9 oz/280 g; 502 yds/459 m)

Sizes XS/S/M L/XL 2/3XL 4/5XL

Blue Moon (29018) 2 3 4 4 O'Gos

Choco-Blueberry (29010) 2 3 4 4 O'Gos

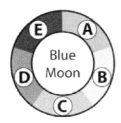 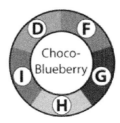

Size U.S. 8 [5 mm] knitting needles. Size U.S. 7 [4.5 mm] circular knitting needle 29" [73.5 cm] long or size needed to obtain gauge.

Yarn needle.

5 (5-6-6) buttons 1" [2.5 cm] in diameter.

Locking stitch marker.

ABBREVIATIONS

Beg = Beginning

Cont = Continue(ity)

K = Knit

P = Purl

Pat = Pattern

Rep = Repeat

RS = Right side

Sp(s) = Space(s)

St(s) = Stitch(es)

Tog = Together

WS = Wrong side

SIZES

To fit bust measurement

XS/S/M 28-38" [71-96.5 cm]

L/XL 40-46" [101.5-117 cm]

2/3XL 48-54" [122-137 cm]

4/5XL 56-62" [142-157.5 cm]

Finished bust measurement

XS/S/M 45" [110 cm]

L/XL 51" [129.5 cm]

2/3XL 57" [145cm]

4/5XL 65" [134.5 cm]

GAUGES

16 sts and 30 rows = 4" in garter st.

17 sts and 23 rows = 4" [10 cm] in stocking st.

INSTRUCTIONS

Notes

• To begin working with the O'Go format, carefully cut plastic tie where the ends of the O'Go meet.

• Pull tie to remove.

• For this pattern, colors can be easily separated by gently pulling apart and cutting at the color transition. Each color is ready to use. Follow color guide shown in Materials section for each O'Go (Contrast A, B, C, D, E, F, G, H and I). Note that Contrast D is in both Blue Moon and Choco-Blueberry O'Gos. You may find it helpful to place each color section in its own resealable (zip lock) bag and label each bag A, B, C, D, E, F, G, H and I.

• Cardigan is worked in patchwork squares joined together as shown in diagrams for Back, Fronts and Sleeves.

• Ribbing, button bands and collar are worked during finishing

Solid Garter Stitch Blocks (make 6 each in B, E and I).

With pair of needles, cast on 22 (25-28-32) sts.

Work in garter st (knit every row), noting 1st row is WS, until work from beg measures 5½ (6-6½-6½)" [14 (15-16.5-16.5) cm], ending on a WS row.

Cast off knitwise (RS).

Striped Garter Stitch Blocks (make 5)

With G and pair of needles, cast on 22 (25-28-32) sts.

Knit 3 rows (garter st), noting 1st row is WS.

With F, knit 2 rows.

With G, knit 2 rows.

Rep last 4 rows until work from beg measures 5½ (6-6½-6½)" [14 (15-16.5-16.5) cm], ending on a WS row.

Cast off knitwise (RS).

Moss Stitch Blocks (make 6 each in A and C)

With pair of needles, cast on 22 (26-28-32) sts.

1st row: (RS). *K1. P1. Rep from * to end of row.

2nd row: As 1st row.

3rd row: *P1. K1. Rep from * to end of row.

4th row: As 3rd row.

Rep last 4 rows until work from beg measures 5½ (6-6½-6½)" [14 (15-16.5-16.5) cm], ending on a WS row.

Cast off knitwise (RS).

Houndstooth Blocks (make 5).

Note: When working from chart, carry yarn not in use loosely across WS of work, but never over more than 3 sts. When it must pass over more than 3 sts, weave it over and under color in use on next st or at center point of sts it passes over. The colors are never twisted around one another.

With A and pair of needles, cast on, cast on 24 (28-32-36) sts.

Work Chart in stocking st, reading knit rows from right to left and purl rows from left to right, noting 4-st rep will be worked 6 (7-8-9) times, until work from beg measures approx 5½ (6-6½-6½)" [14 (15-16.5-

16.5) cm], ending on Row 4 of chart.

With H, cast off knitwise (RS).

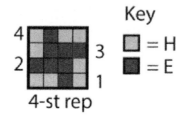

Broken Rib Squares (make 5 each in H and G).

With pair of needles, cast on 23 (25-31-35) sts.

1st row: (RS). Knit.

2nd row: K1. *P1. K1. Rep from * to end of row.

Rep last 2 rows until work from beg measures 5½ (6-6½-6½)" [14 (15-16.5-16.5) cm], ending on a WS row.

Cast off knitwise (RS).

Collar

With C and circular needle, cast on 94 (102-110-110) sts. Do not join.

Work back and forth across needle in rows as follows:

1st row: (RS). *K2. P2. Rep from * to last 2 sts. K2.

2nd row: *P2. K2. Rep from * to last 2 sts. P2.

Rep last 2 rows of (K2. P2) ribbing for 8" [20.5 cm].

Cast off in rib.

Cuff Ribbing

With F and circular needle, cast on 70 (74-82-94) sts. Do not join.

Work back and forth across needle in rows as follows:

Work in (K2. P2) ribbing as given for Collar for 2" [5 cm], ending on a WS row.

Cast off in rib.

Bottom Ribbing

With D and circular needle, cast on 190 (214-238-272) sts. Do not join.

Work back and forth across needle in rows as follows:

Work in (K2. P2) ribbing as given for Collar for 2" [5 cm], ending on a WS row.

Cast off in rib.

Buttonhole Band

With D and circular needle cast on 102 (110-124-124) sts. Do not join.

Work back and forth across needle in rows as follows:

Work in (K2. P2) ribbing as given for Collar for 1" [2.5 cm], ending on a WS row.

Buttonhole row: (RS). K2. Cast off next 2 sts. *Rib next 22 (24-22-22) sts. Cast off next 2 sts. Rep from * to last 2 sts. K2.

Next row: Work in (K2. P2) ribbing, casting on 2 sts over cast off sts. Cont in (K2. P2) ribbing until Band measures 2" [5 cm].

Cast off in rib.

Button Band: Work as given for Buttonhole Band, omitting references to buttonholes.

Finishing

Following Assembly Diagrams in the end, with WS facing each other, sew Motifs tog, using mattress st.

Place markers 6 (7-8-10)" [15 (18-20.5-25.5) cm] in from side edges of Fronts and Back for shoulders.

Sew shoulder seams. Sew Collar around neck edge.

Place markers at sides of Fronts and Back for Sleeves 8¼ (9¼-10½-

12)" [21 (23.5-25.5-30.5) cm] down from shoulders. Sew in sleeves between markers.

Sew Cuff Ribbing to end of Sleeves. Sew side and sleeve seams. Sew Bottom Ribbing to lower edge of Cardigan.

Sew buttonhole and button band to front edge of Cardigan, making note of which side you want buttons and buttonholes on, respectively. Sew buttons onto button band to correspond to buttonholes.

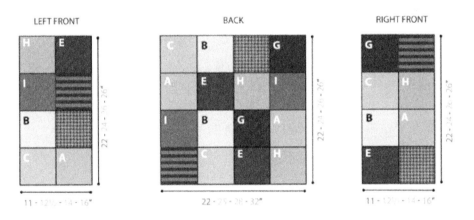

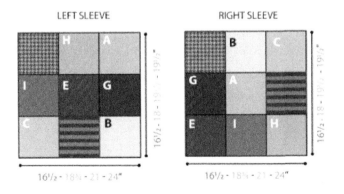

Striped Cardigan

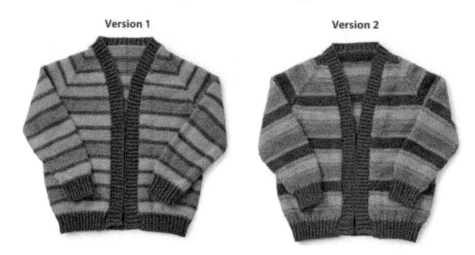

MATERIALS

Caron® x Pantone™ (3.5 oz/100 g; 127 yds/116m)

Sizes	XS/S	M	L	XL	2/3 XL	4/5 XL
Dance Party (01029)	6	7	8	9	11	13 braids

Version 1

A - 18-2436	B - 18-3520	C - 17-4540	D - 19-4324	E - 19-4009

Version 2

A - 19-4009	B - 17-4540	C - 18-3520	D - 18-2436	E - 19-4324

Sizes U.S. 9 [5.5 mm] and U.S. 10 [6 mm] circular knitting needles 29"

[73.5 cm] long.

Sets of 4 sizes U.S. 9 (5.5 mm) and U.S. 10 (6 mm) double-pointed knitting needles or sizes needed to obtain gauge.

4 stitch markers.

2 stitch holders.

ABBREVIATIONS

Approx = Approximately

Beg = Beginning

Cont = Continue(ity)

K = Knit

K1tbl = Knit next stitch through back loop

K2tog = Knit next 2 stitches together

M1L = Make 1 stitch by picking up horizontal loop lying before next stitch from front to back and knitting into back of loop.

M1R = Make 1 stitch by picking up horizontal loop lying before next stitch from back to front and knitting into front of loop

P = Purl

Pat = Pattern

P1tbl = Purl next stitch through back loop

PM = Place marker

Rem = Remain(ing)

Rep = Repeat

RS = Right side

SM = Slip marker

Ssk = Slip next 2 stitches knitwise one at a time. Pass them back on to left-hand needle, then knit through back loops together

WS = Wrong side

SIZES

To fit bust measurement

XS/S 28-34" [71-86.5 cm]

M 36-38" [91.5-96.5 cm]

L 40-42" [101.5-106.5 cm]

XL 44-46" [112-117 cm]

2/3 XL 48-54" [122-137 cm]

4/5 XL 56-62" [142-157.5 cm]

Finished bust measurement

XS/S 36" [91.5 cm]

M 40" [101.5 cm]

L 44" [112 cm]

XL 48" [122 cm]

2/3 XL 56" [142 cm]

4/5 XL 64" [162.5 cm]

GAUGE

15 sts and 20 rows = 4" [10 cm] in stocking st with larger needles.

INSTRUCTIONS

Notes:

• Before working with Caron® x Pantone™ multi-shade yarn braid, separate each color link and wind into 5 separate balls.

• Each color link will be referenced by its Pantone # (see ball band).

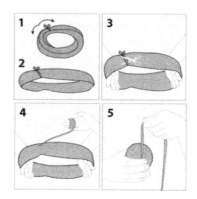

• Designate each different shade of the 5 separate yarn balls as Contrast A, B, C, D and E as noted in Materials section (or as desired).

• Due to finite amount of yarn in each shade, pattern gauge must be matched to ensure successful results.

• Garment is intended to be worn open at center front. The instructions are written for smallest size. If changes are necessary for larger sizes the instructions will be written thus ( ). When only one number is given, it applies to all sizes.

Stripe Pat

With A, work 6 rows.

With D, work 2 rows.

With B, work 6 rows.

With D, work 2 rows.

With C, work 6 rows.

With D, work 2 rows.

These 24 rows form Stripe Pat.

Note: Contrast E is reserved for ribbing.

Body is worked in one piece on circular needle. Sleeves are worked in the round on double-pointed needles.

BODY

Beg at neck edge, with A and larger circular needle, cast on 35 (39-41-43-51-55) sts.

Set Up Row: K3. PM. K2. PM. K25 (29-31-33-41-45). PM. K2. PM. Knit to end of row.

Next row: Purl.

Begin Raglan Increases:

1st row: (Knit to 1 st before marker. M1R. K1. SM. K1. M1L) 4 times. Knit to end of row. 43 (47-49-51-59-63) sts.

2nd and alt rows: Purl.

3rd row: As 1st row. 51 (55-57-59-67-71) sts.

5th row: K2. M1L. (Knit to 1 st before marker. M1R. K1. SM. K1. M1L) 4 times. Knit to last 2 sts. M1R. K2. 61 (65-67-69-77-81) sts.

6th row: Purl.

First 8 rows of Stripe Pat are complete. Keeping cont of Stripe Pat, rep 1st to 6th rows 5 (6-6-7-7-8) times more, ending last rep on a 6th (2nd-6th-2nd-6th-6th) row. 191 (203-223-233-259-289) sts.

Divide Body and Sleeves

Next row: K27 (28-31-32-35-39). Place next 38 (40-44-46-50-56) sts on st holder. Cast on 6 (8-10-12-16-18) sts. K61 (67-73-77-89-99). Place next 38 (40-44-46-50-56) sts on st holder. Cast on 6 (8-10-12-16-18) sts. Knit to end of row. 127 (139-155-165-191-213) Body sts.

Cont in Stripe Pat until Body from joining row measures approx 12 (12-12½-13-13½-14)" [30.5 (30.5-3 2-3 3-34.5-35.5) cm], ending on a 6th, 14th, or 22nd row of Stripe Pat.

Bottom Ribbing

Change to E and smaller circular needle.

1st row: (RS). K1tbl. *P1tbl. K1tbl. Rep from * to end of row.

2nd row: P1tbl. *K1tbl. P1tbl. Rep from * to end of row.

Rep these 2 rows for Twisted Rib Pat for 2" [5 cm], ending on a RS row. Cast off in pat.

SLEEVES

With set of 4 larger double-pointed needles, using appropriate color to cont in Stripe Pat, beg at center of underarm, pick up and knit 3 (4-5-6-8-9) sts. K38 (40-44-46-50-56) from st holder. Pick up and knit 3 (4-5-6-8-9) sts across rem of underarm cast on edge. Join in rnd. PM on first st. 44 (48-54-58-66-74) sts.

Keeping cont of Stripe Pat, work in rnds until Sleeve measures 7 (6½-6-5½-5-4)" [18 (16.5-15-14-12.5-10) cm] from underarm

Shape sides: 1st rnd: K1. K2tog. Knit to last 3 sts. ssk. K1. 42 (46-52-56-64-72) sts.

2nd to 4th rnds: Knit.

Rep these 4 rnds 3 (4-6-7-7-9) times more. 36 (38-40-42-50-54) sts.

Cont even in Stripe Pat until Sleeve from underarm measures approx 12 (12-11½-11-11-11)" [30.5 (30.5-29-28-28-25.5) cm], ending on a 6th, 14th, or 22nd row of Stripe Pat.

Ribbing

Change to E and smaller doublepointed needles.

1st rnd: *K1tbl. P1tbl. Rep from * around.

Rep last rnd until ribbing measures 2" [5 cm]. Cast off in ribbing.

Neckband

With smaller circular needle and E, pick up and knit 100 (104-110-114-118-122) sts up along Right Front to Sleeve; 29 (33-35-37-45-49) sts across top of Sleeves and Back neck edge; and 100 (104-110-114-118-122) sts down Left Front. 229 (241-255-265-281-293) sts

1st row: (WS). P1tbl. *K1tbl. P1tbl. Rep from * to end of row.

2nd row: K1tbl. *P1tbl. K1tbl. Rep from * to end of row.

Rep these 2 rows for Twisted Rib Pat for 1½" [4 cm], ending on a RS row. Cast off in pat.

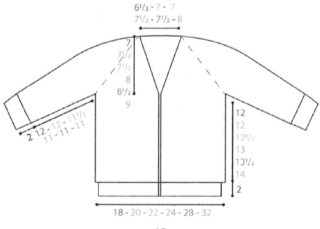

Cable Cardigan

MATERIALS

Bernat® Softee Chunky Tweeds™ (10.5 oz/300 g; 316 yds/289 m)

Sizes XS/S M L XL 2/3XL 4/5XL

Soft Gray Tweed (11004) 3 3 4 4 5 5 balls

Sizes U.S. 10½ (6.5 mm) and U.S. 11 (8 mm) circular knitting needles 29" [73.5 cm] long.

Set of 4 sizes U.S. 10½ (6.5 mm) and U.S. 11 (8 mm) double-pointed knitting needles or sizes needed to obtain gauge.

Cable needle.

2 stitch markers.

Stitch holder.

6 buttons.

ABBREVIATIONS

Approx = Approximately

Beg = Begin(ning)

C6B = Slip next 3 stitches onto cable needle and leave at back of work. K3, then K3 from cable needle

C6F = Slip next 3 stitches onto cable needle and leave at front of work. K3, then K3 from cable needle

Cont = Continue(ity)

K = Knit

K2tog = Knit next 2 stitches together

M1L = Make 1 stitch by picking up horizontal loop lying before next stitch from front to back and knitting into back of loop.

M1R = Make 1 stitch by picking up horizontal loop lying before next stitch from back to front and knitting into front of loop

P = Purl

Pat = Pattern

P2tog = Purl next 2 stitches together

P2togtbl = Purl next 2 stitches together through back loops

PM = Place marker

Rem = Remain(ing)

Rep = Repeat

Rnd(s) = Round(s)

RS = Right side

SM = Slip marker

Ssk = Slip next 2 sitches one at a time. Pass them back onto left-hand needle, then knit through the back loops together.

St(s) = Stitch(es)

WS = Wrong side

Yo = Yarn over

SIZES

To fit bust measurement

XS/S 28-34" [71-86.5 cm]

M 36-38" [91.5-96.5 cm]

L 40-42" [101.5-106.5 cm]

XL 44-46" [112-117 cm]

2/3XL 48-54" [122-137 cm]

4/5XL 56-62" [142-157.5 cm]

Finished bust measurement

XS/S 37" [94 cm]

M 41½" [105.5 cm]

L 46" [117 cm]

XL 49" [124.5 cm]

2/3XL 57½" [146 cm]

4/5XL 62" [157.5 cm]

GAUGE

11 sts and 14 rows = 4" [10 cm] in stocking st on larger needles.

INSTRUCTIONS

The instructions are written for smallest size. If changes are necessary for larger size(s) the instructions will be written thus ( ). When only one number is given, it applies to all sizes.

Right Cable Panel (worked over 8 sts). See chart at the end.

1st row: P1. C6F. P1.

2nd row: K1. P6. K1.

3rd row: P1. K6. P1.

4th row: As 2nd row.

5th to 8th rows: Rep 3rd and 4th rows twice.

These 8 rows form Right Cable Panel.

Left Cable Panel (worked over 8 sts). See chart at the end.

1st row: P1. C6B. P1.

2nd row: K1. P6. K1.

3rd row: P1. K6. P1.

4th row: As 2nd row.

5th to 8th rows: Rep 3rd and 4th rows twice.

These 8 rows form Left Cable Panel.

Note: Body is worked in one piece to armholes. Sleeves are worked in the round until the cap shaping, then they are worked back and forth in rows to top.

BODY

With smaller circular needle,cast on 98 (110-122-130-154-166) sts.

1st row: (RS). K2. *P2. K2. Rep from * across.

2nd row: P2. *K2. P2. Rep from * across.

Rep last 2 rows (K2. P2) ribbing for 2½" [6.5 cm], ending on a WS row.

Change to larger circular needle and proceed as follows:

1st row: K9 (9-11-11-12-12). Work 1st row of Right Cable Panel across next 8 sts. Knit to last 17 (17-19-19-20-20) sts. Work 1st row of Left Cable Panel across next 8 sts. K9 (9-11-11-12-12).

2nd row: P9 (9-11-11-12-12). Work 2nd row of Left Cable Panel across next 8 sts. Purl to last 17 (17-19-19-20-20) sts. Work 2nd row of Right Cable Panel across next 8 sts. P9 (9-11-11-12-12).

Cable Panels are now in position. Cont in pat, keeping cont of Cable Panels, until work from beg measures 18½" [42 cm], ending on a WS row.

Keeping cont of Cable Panels, begin front shaping:

1st row: (RS). K1. ssk. Pat to last 3 sts. K2tog. K1. 96 (108-120-128-152-164) sts.

2nd row: Work even in pat.

Divide for Right Front: 1st row: K1. ssk. Pat across next 18 (20-23-24-28-29) sts. Turn. Leave rem sts on spare needle. 20 (22-25-26-30-31) sts for Right Front.

Next row: Work even in pat.

Sizes XS/S, M, L, XL only:

1st row: K1. ssk. Pat to last 3 sts. K2tog. K1. 18 (20-23-24) sts.

2nd row: Work even in pat.

3rd row: Pat to last 3 sts. K2tog. K1. 17 (19-22-23) sts.

4th row: As 2nd row.

Sizes M, L and XL only: Rep last 4 rows once more. (16-19-20) sts.

Sizes XS/S, L and XL only: Next row: K1. ssk. Pat to last 3 sts. K2tog. K1. 15 (17-18) sts.

Sizes 2/3XL and 4/5XL only:

1st row: K1. ssk. Pat to last 3 sts. K2tog. K1. (28-29) sts.

2nd row: P1. P2tog. Pat to end of row. (27-28) sts.

3rd row: Pat to last 3 sts. K2tog. K1. (26-27) sts.

4th row: P1. P2tog. Pat to end of row. (25-26) sts.

5th row: As 1st row. (23-24) sts.

6th row: Work even in pat.

7th row: Pat to last 3 sts. K2tog. K1. (22-23) sts.

8th row: As 6th row.

9th row: As 1st row. (20-21) sts.

10th row: As 6th row.

Sizes XS/S, L, XL, 2/3XL and 4/5XL only: Work 2 rows even in pat.

All Sizes: 1st row: (RS). K1. ssk. Pat to end of row. 14 (15-16-17-19-20) sts.

2nd to 4th rows: Work even in pat.

Rep last 4 rows until 11 (12-12-12-13-14) sts rem.

Cont even in pat until armhole measures 8 (8-9-9½-10-10½)" [20.5 (20.5-23-24-25.5-26.5) cm], ending on a RS row.

Shape shoulder: Cast off 5 (6-6-6-7-7) sts at beg of next row.

Purl 1 row.

Cast off rem 6 (6-6-6-6-7) sts.

Back: With larger circular needle, join yarn to next unworked st.

Next row: (RS). Cast o 6 (8-8-10-14-16) sts. K42 (46-52-54-62-68) (including rem st on needle after cast off). Turn. Leave rem sts on spare needle.

Next row: Purl. 42 (46-52-54-62-68) sts.

Sizes XS/S, M, L and XL only:

49

1st row: (RS). K1. ssk. Knit to last 3 sts. K2tog. K1. 40 (44-50-52) sts.

2nd row: Purl.

Rep these 2 rows until 36 (38-42-44) sts rem, ending on a WS row.

Sizes 2/3XL and 4/5XL only:

1st row: K1. ssk. Knit to last 3 sts. K2tog. K1. (60-66) sts.

2nd row: P1. P2tog. Purl to last 3 sts. P2togtbl. P1. (58-64) sts.

3rd row: As 1st row. (56-62) sts.

4th row: As 2nd row. (54-60) sts.

5th row: As 1st row. (52-58) sts.

6th row: Purl.

7th row: As 1st row. (50-56) sts.

8th row: Purl.

9th row: As 1st row. (48-54) sts.

10th row: Purl.

All sizes: Cont even in stocking st until armhole measures 8 (8-9-9½-10-10½)" [20.5 (20.5-23-24-25.5-26.5) cm], ending on a WS row.

Shape shoulders: Cast off 5 (6-6-6-7-7) sts at beg of next 2 rows, then 6 (6-6-6-6-7) sts at beg of following 2 rows.

Leave rem 14 (14-18-20-22-26) sts on a st holder.

Left Front: With larger circular needle, join yarn to next unworked st.

1st row: (RS). Cast off 6 (8-8-10-14-16) sts. Pat to last 3 sts. K2tog. K1. 20 (22-25-26-30-31) sts.

2nd row: Work even in pat.

Sizes XS/S, M, L and XL only:

1st row: K1. ssk. Pat to last 3 sts. K2tog. K1. 18 (20-23-24) sts.

2nd row: Work even in pat.

3rd row: K1. ssk. Pat to end of row. 17 (19-22-23) sts.

4th row: As 2nd row.

Sizes M, L and XL only: Rep last 4 rows once more. (16-19-20) sts.

Size XS/S, L and XL only: Next row: K1. ssk. Pat to last 3 sts. K2tog. K1. 15 (17-18) sts.

Sizes 2/3XL and 4/5XL only:

1st row: K1. ssk. Pat to last 3 sts. K2tog. K1. (28-29) sts.

2nd row: Pat to last 3 sts. P2togtbl. P1. (27-28) sts.

3rd row: K1. ssk. Pat to end of row. (26-27) sts.

4th row: As 2nd row. (25-26) sts.

5th row: As 1st row. (23-24) sts.

6th row: Work even in pat.

7th row: K1. ssk. Pat to end of row. (22-23) sts.

8th row: As 6th row.

9th row: As 1st row. (20-21) sts.

10th row: As 6th row.

Sizes XS/S, L, XL, 2/3XL and 4/5XL only: Work 2 rows even in pat.

All Sizes: 1st row: (RS). Pat to last 3 sts. K2tog. K1. 14 (15-16-17 -18) sts.

2nd to 4th rows: Work even in pat. Rep last 4 rows until 11 (12-12-12-13-14) sts rem.

Cont even in pat until armhole measures 8 (8-9-9½-10-10½)" [20.5 (20.5-23-24-25.5-26.5 cm], ending on a WS row.

Shape shoulder: Cast off 5 (6-6-6-7-7) sts at beg of next row.

Knit 1 row.

Cast off rem 6 (6-6-6-6-7) sts.

SLEEVES

With smaller double-pointed needles, cast on 24 (24-28-28-32-32) sts. Divide sts onto 3 needles and join in rnd, PM on first st.

1st rnd: *K2. P2. Rep from * around.

Rep last rnd of (K2. P2) ribbing for 2½" [6.5 cm].

Change to larger set of doublepointed needles and knit 2 rnds.

Begin Sleeve Increases

Inc rnd: K1. M1L. Knit to last st. M1R. K1. 26 (26-30-30-34-34) sts.

Rep inc rnd every following 6th (5th-5th-4th-4th-3rd) rnd 6 (8-7-9-9-11) times more. 38 (42-44-48-52-56) sts.

Cont even until Sleeve from beg measures 18 (18-17-16½-16½-16)" [45.5 (45.5-43-42-42-40.5) cm].

Next rnd: Knit to last 3 (3-4-5-6-7) sts. Bind off next 6 (6-8-10-12-14) sts. 32 (36-36-38-40-42) sts.

Working back and forth in rows, proceed as follows:

1st row: (RS). K1. ssk. Knit to last 3 sts. K2tog. K1. 30 (34-34-36-38-40) sts.

2nd row: Purl.

Rep these 2 rows to 18 (18-18-22-22-22) sts, ending on a WS row.

Next row: (RS). ssk. Knit to last 2 sts. K2tog.

Next row: P2tog. Purl to last 2 sts. P2togtbl.

Rep last 2 rows to 6 sts. Cast off.

FINISHING

Sew shoulder seams. Sew in Sleeves.

Button and Buttonhole Band:

With RS facing and smaller circular needle, pick up and knit 72 (72-74-75-78-80) sts up Right Front to shoulder seam. K14 (14-18-20-22-26) from Back st holder. Pick up and knit 72 (72-74-75-78-80) sts down Left Front edge to cast on edge. 158 (158-166-170-178-186) sts.

1st row: (WS). *P2. K2. Rep from * to last 2 sts. P2.

2nd row: *K2. P2. Rep from * to last 2 sts. K2.

3rd row: As 1st row.

4th row: K2. P2tog. yo. (K2. P2. K2. P2tog. yo) 5 times. *K2. P2. Rep from * to last 2 sts. K2.

5th and 6th rows: As 1st and 2nd rows.

Cast off in ribbing.

Sew buttons to left side of button band to correspond to buttonholes.

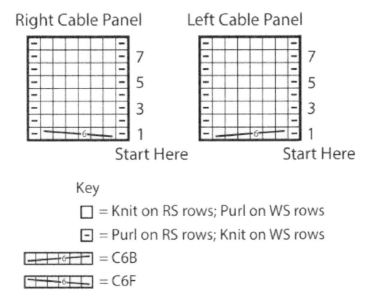

Right Cable Panel   Left Cable Panel

Start Here   Start Here

Key
☐ = Knit on RS rows; Purl on WS rows
⊟ = Purl on RS rows; Knit on WS rows
= C6B
= C6F

Knit Cardigan

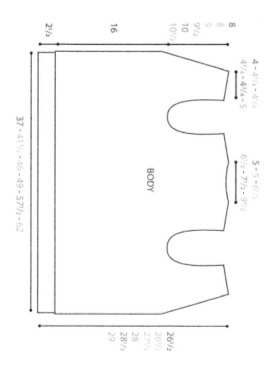

BODY

2½

16

8
8
9½
10
10½

4 - 4¼ - 4¼
4¼ - 4¾ - 5

5 - 5 - 6½
6½ - 7½ - 9½

37 - 41½ - 46 - 49 - 57½ - 62

26½
26½
27½
28
28½
29

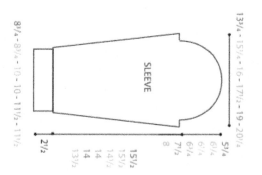

SLEEVE

2½

8¾ - 8¾ - 10 - 10 - 11½ - 11½

13¾ - 15½ - 16 - 17½ - 19 - 20½

5¾
6¼
6¼
6¾
7½
8

15½
15½
14½
14
14
13½

Cozy Long Cardigan

MATERIALS

RED HEART® Collage™: 11 (13, 14, 15, 16) balls 9980 Forget-Me-Not

Susan Bates® Circular Knitting Needles: 12.75mm [US 17] 29" (73.5 cm)

Yarn needle

ABBREVIATIONS

k = knit;

k2tog = knit next 2 sts together;

p = purl;

st(s) = stitch(es);

[ ] = work directions in brackets the number of times specified;

* or ** = repeat whatever follows the * or ** as indicated.

GAUGE: 7 sts = 4" (10 cm); 10 rows = 4" (10 cm) in Stockinette st. CHECK YOUR GAUGE. Use any size needles to obtain the gauge.

Directions are for size Small. Changes for sizes Medium, Large, Extra Large, and 2X are in parentheses.

Cardigan measures 39 (42½, 47, 50½, 55)" (99 (108, 119.5, 128.5, 139.5) cm) around bust and 34½ (35½, 35½, 36½, 36½)" in length.

NOTES

1. Back, Left Front, and Right Front are worked from bottom edges upwards and sewn together.

2. The two Sleeves are worked from top down and sewn to body.

3. Circular needle is used to accommodate the width of the fabric and thickness of the yarn. Work back and forth in rows as if working with straight needles.

SPECIAL STITCHES

ssk = slip next two stitches knitwise one at a time to right needle, insert point of left needle through front of sts, knit these sts together through back loop.

1 x 1 RIB

When worked over an odd number of sts:

Row 1 (right side): K1, * p1, k1; repeat from * to end.

Row 2: P1, * k1, p1; repeat from * to end.

Repeat Rows 1 and 2 for 1 x 1 Rib.

When worked over an even number of sts:

Every Row: * K1, p1; repeat from * to end.

BACK

Cast on 44 (47, 51, 54, 58) sts.

Work in 1 x 1 ribbing for 5 rows.

Next row (wrong side): Purl.

Next row: Knit.

Continue in Stockinette st until piece measures 20" (51 cm) from cast on edge, ending after a wrong side (purl) row.

Shape Sides

Next row (decrease row, right side): K1, k2tog, knit to last 3 sts, ssk, k1 – 42 (45, 49, 52, 56) sts. [Work 3 rows evenly, then repeat decrease row] twice – 38 (41, 45, 48, 52) sts.

Purl 1 row, repeat decrease row once more, then purl 1 more row – 36 (39, 43, 46, 50) sts.

Shape Armholes

Row 1 (right side): Bind off 4 (5, 6, 7, 8) sts, knit to end – 32 (34, 37, 39, 42) sts.

Row 2: Bind off 4 (5, 6, 7, 8) sts, purl to end – 28 (29, 31, 32, 34) sts.

Work evenly until armholes measure 9 (10, 10, 11, 11)" (23 (25.5, 25.5, 28, 28) cm), ending with after wrong side row.

Bind off all sts.

LEFT FRONT

Cast on 20 (22, 24, 26, 28) sts.

Row 1 (right side): Work in 1 x 1 Rib to last 3 sts, k3.

Row 2: K3, work in 1 x 1 Rib to end.

Repeat Rows 1 and 2 once more, then Row 1 only once more.

Next 2 rows:

Row 1 (wrong side): K3, purl to end.

Row 2: Knit.

Repeat the last 2 rows until piece measures 20" (51 cm) from cast on edge, ending after a wrong side row

Shape Side

Next row (decrease row, right side): K1, k2tog, knit to end – 19 (21, 23, 25, 27) sts.

[Work 3 rows evenly, then repeat decrease row] twice – 17 (19, 21, 23, 25) sts.

Work 1 row evenly, repeat decrease row once more, then work one more row evenly – 16 (18, 20, 22, 24) sts.

Shape Armhole

Row 1 (right side): Bind off 4 (5, 6, 7, 8) sts, knit to end – 12 (13, 14, 15, 16) sts.

Row 2: K3, purl to end of row.

Row 3: Knit.

Repeat rows 2 and 3 until armhole measures 9 (10, 10, 11, 11)" (23 (25.5, 25.5, 28, 28) cm), ending after a wrong side row.

Collar Extension

Row 1 (right side): Bind off 9 (10, 11, 12, 13) sts, knit to end – 3 sts.

Work evenly in Garter st for 3" (7.5 cm), then bind off all sts.

RIGHT FRONT

Cast on 20 (22, 24, 26, 28) sts.

Row 1 (right side): K3, work in 1 x 1 Rib to end.

Row 2: Work in 1 x 1 Rib to last 3 sts, k3.

Repeat Rows 1 and 2 once more, then Row 1 only once more.

Next 2 rows:

Row 1 (wrong side): Purl to last 3 sts, k3.

Row 2: Knit.

Repeat the last 2 rows until piece measures 20" (51 cm) from cast on edge, ending after a wrong side row.

Shape Side

Next row (decrease row, right side):

Knit to last 3 sts, ssk, k1 – 19 (21, 23, 25, 27) sts.

[Work 3 rows evenly, then repeat decrease row] twice – 17 (19, 21, 23, 25) sts.

Work 1 row evenly, then repeat decrease row once more – 16 (18, 20, 22, 24) sts.

Shape Armhole

Row 1 (wrong side): Bind off 4 (5, 6, 7, 8) sts, purl to last 3 sts, k3 –12 (13, 14, 15, 16) sts.

Row 2: Knit.

Row 3: Purl to last 3 sts, k3.

Repeat rows 2 and 3 until armhole measures 9 (10, 10, 11, 11)" (23 (25.5, 25.5, 28, 28) cm), ending after a right side row.

Collar Extension

Row 1 (wrong side): Bind off 9 (10, 11, 12, 13) sts, knit to end – 3 sts.

Work evenly in Garter st for 3" (7.5 cm), then bind off all sts.

SLEEVES (make 2)

Cast on 30 (34, 34, 38, 38) sts, and work 15 rows in 1 x 1 Rib.

Next row (decrease row, right side): K1, k2tog, knit to last 3 sts, ssk, k1 – 28 (32, 32, 36, 36) sts.

Repeat this decrease every 4 rows 4 more times – 20 (24, 24, 28, 28) sts. Work evenly until piece measures 15" (38 cm) from beginning.

Work in 1 x 1 Rib for 2" (5 cm), then bind off all sts.

FINISHING

Sew shoulder seams.

Sew bound off edges of collar extensions together.

Sew lower edge of collar to back neck, easing to fit.

Sew side and sleeve seams. Sew sleeves into armholes.

Weave in all loose ends.

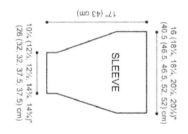

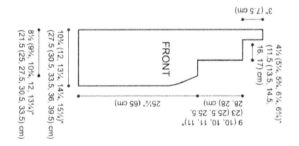

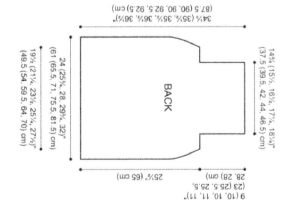

Fair Isle Yoke Cardigan

MATERIALS

Caron® x Pantone™ (3.5 oz /100 g; 127 yds/116 m)

Sizes XS/S M L XL 2/3XL 4/5XL

Knit Cardigan

Main Color (MC) Midnight Blue (01004) 6 7 9 10 12 14 braids

Contrast A Lapis (01025) 1 1 1 1 2 2 braid(s)

Contrast B Frozen Berry (01022) 2 2 2 2 3 3 braids

MC - 19-4044				
A - 17-5034				
B1 - 13-4103	B2 - 17-5034	B3 - 17-4540	B4 - 18-2929	B5 - 19-4044

Sizes U.S. 9 (5.5 mm) and U.S. 10 (6 mm) circular knitting needles 29" [75 cm] long.

Set of 4 sizes U.S. 9 (5.5 mm) and U.S. 10 (6 mm) doublepointed knitting needles or size needed to obtain gauge.

Stitch marker.

4 st holders.

6 buttons - 5/8" [1.5 cm] diameter.

ABBREVIATIONS

Beg = Begin(ning)

Cont = Continue(ity)

Dec = Decrease(ing)

Inc = Increase(ing)

K = Knit

K2tog = Knit next 2 stitches together

M1 = Make 1 stitch by picking up horizontal loop lying before next stitch and knitting into back of loop

P = Purl

Rem = Remaining

Rep = Repeat

Rnd(s) = Round(s)

RS = Right side

Sl1K = Slip next stitch knitwise

Sl1P = Slip next stitch purlwise

St(s) = Stitch(es)

Tog = Together

WS = Wrong side

Yo = Yarn over

SIZES

To fit bust measurement

XS/S 28-34" [71-86.5 cm]

M 36-38" [91.5-96.5 cm]

L 40-42" [101.5-106.5 cm]

XL 44-46" [112-117 cm]

2/3 XL 48-54" [122-137 cm]

4/5 XL 56-62" [142-157.5 cm]

Finished bust

XS/S 37" [94 cm]

M 40" [101.5 cm]

L 44" [112 cm]

XL 48" [122 cm]

2/3 XL 57" [145 cm]

4/5 XL 65" [165 cm]

GAUGE

15 sts and 20 rows = 4" [10 cm] in stocking st with larger needles.

INSTRUCTIONS

The instructions are written for smallest size. If changes are necessary for larger size(s) the instructions will be written thus ( ). When only one number is given, it applies to all sizes.

Notes:

• Before working with Caron® x Pantone™ multi-shade yarn braid, separate each color link and wind into 5 separate balls.

• Each color link will be referenced by its colour number (see label)

• Designate each different shade of the 5 separate yarn balls as Colors 1, 2, 3, 4 and 5 as noted in Materials section (or as desired).

• Due to finite amount of yarn in each shade, pattern gauge must be matched to ensure successful results

• When working from chart, carry yarn not in use loosely across WS of work but never over more than 5 sts. When it must pass over more than 5 sts, weave it over and under color not in use. The colors are never twisted around one another.

BODY

Note: Body is worked in 1 piece to armholes.

Knit Cardigan

With MC and smaller circular needle, cast on 138 (150-166-182-214-246) sts. Do not join.

Work back and forth across needle as follows:

1st row: (RS). K2. *P2. K2. Rep from * to end of row.

2nd row: P2. *K2. P2. Rep from * to end of row.

Rep last 2 rows of (K2. P2) ribbing for 3" [7.5 cm].

Change to larger circular needle and work in stocking st until work from beg measures 16" [40.5 cm], ending on a purl row.

Shape Front (short-turn rows):

Next row: (RS). K124 (135-148-162-191-220). Sl1P. Turn.

Next row: Sl1P. P110 (120-130-142-168-194). Sl1. Turn.

Next row: Sl1K. K105 (114-123-134-158-182). Sl1P. Turn.

Next row: Sl1P. P100 (108-116-126-148-170). Sl1K. Turn.

Next row: Sl1K. K95 (102-109-118-138-158). Sl1P. Turn.

Next row: Sl1P. P90 (96-102-110-128-146). Sl1K. Turn.

Note: To avoid a hole when knitting a slipped st, pick up the st below the slipped st and slip it onto left hand needle. Knit this st tog with slipped st above.

Next row: Sl1K. Knit to end of row.

Next row: Purl all sts.

Next row: Knit.

Next row: (WS).P38 (41-46-50-59-67). Slip last 8 (8-10-10-12-12) sts onto st holder (armhole). P70 (76-84-92-108-124). Slip last 8 (8-10-10-12-12) sts onto st holder (armhole). Knit to end of row.

Leave rem Body sts on a st holder.

SLEEVES

With MC and set of 4 smaller double-pointed needles, cast on 40 (40-44-44-48-48) sts. Join in rnd and divide sts onto 3 needles, placing a marker on first st.

1st rnd: *K2. P2. Rep from * around. Rep last rnd of (K2. P2) ribbing for 4" [10 cm].

Change to larger set of needles.

Knit in rnds, inc 1 st at beg and end of 2nd and every following 10th (8th-8th-6th-6th-4th) rnd to 50 (44-48-58-62-62) sts, then every following 12th (10th-10th-8th8th-6th) rnd to 52 (54-58-62-66-70) sts.

Cont even until work from beg measures 18 (18-18-17½-17½-16½)" [45.5 (45.5-45.5-44.5-44.5-42) cm].

Next rnd: K4 (4-5-5-6-6). Slip these 4 (4-5-5-6-6) sts and last 4 (4-5-5-6-6) sts onto a safety pin for armhole. K44 (46-48-52-54-58). Break yarn leaving an end 18" [45.5 cm] long for grafting at underarm. Leave sts on a spare needle.

YOKE

1st row: (RS). With MC, K30 (33-36-40-47-55) of Right Front. K44 (46-48-52-54-58) of Right Sleeve. K62 (68-74-82-96-120) of Back. K44 (46-48-52-54-58) of Left Sleeve. Knit to end of row. 210 (226-242-266-298-338) sts.

2nd row: Purl.

Sizes XS/S, M, 2/3XL and 4/5XL only: Next row: [K33 (113-149-169). M1] 6 (2-2-2) times. Knit to end of row. 216 (228-300-336) sts.

Sizes L and XL only: Next row: [K(119-131). K2tog] twice. (240-264) sts.

All sizes: Next row: Purl.

Work Chart I (I-I-II-II-II) in fair isle to end of chart, reading knit rows from right to left and purl rows from left to right, working 12-st rep

18 (19-20-22-25-28) times. 72 (76-80-88-100-112) sts. Break all contrast colors.

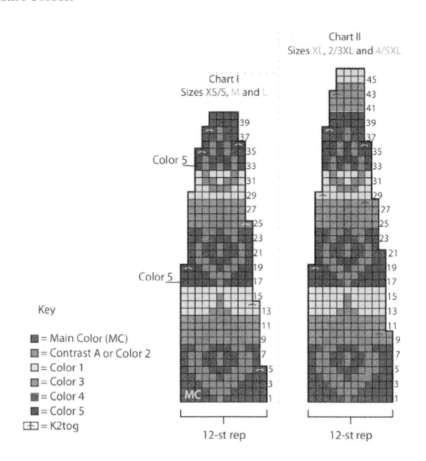

Cont with A only.

Beg with a knit row, work 2 rows in stocking st.

Next row: K8 (8-9-10-11-13). K2tog. *K16 (17-18-20-23-26). K2tog. Rep from * to last 8 (9-9-10-12-13) sts. K8 (9-9-10-12-13). 68 (72-76-

84-96-108) sts.

Next row: Purl.

Sizes M, L, XL, 2/3XL and 4/5XL only: Next row: K(8-9-9-11-12). K2tog. *K(16-17-19-22-25). K2tog. Rep from * to last (8-9-10-11-13) sts. K(8-9-10-11-13). (68-72-80-92-104) sts.

Next row: Purl.

Sizes XL, 2/3XL and 4/5XL only: Next row: K(9-11-8). K2tog. *K(18-21-10). K2tog. Rep from * to last (9-10-10) sts. K(9-10-10). (76-88-96) sts.

Next row: Purl.

Sizes 2/3XL and 4/5XL only: Next row: K(10-2). K2tog. *K(20-4). K2tog. Rep from * to last (10-2) sts. K(10-2). 80 sts.

Next row: Purl.

All sizes: Next row: (RS). Knit, dec 2 sts evenly across. 66 (66-70-74-78-78) sts.

Change to smaller needles and work 2" [5 cm] in (K2. P2) ribbing as given for Body. Cast off in rib.

Graft underarm seams.

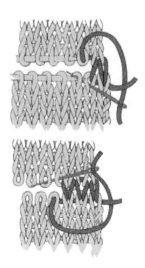

Button band: With RS facing, MC and smaller circular needle, pick up and knit 90 (90-90-92-96-96) sts evenly along left side of Cardigan.

Knit 4 rows. Cast off knitwise (WS).

Buttonhole Band: With RS facing, MC and smaller circular needle, pick up and knit 90 (90-90-92-96-96) sts evenly along right side of Cardigan.

1st row: (WS). Knit.

2nd row: K3 (3-3-4-3-3). *yo. K2tog. K12 (12-12-12-13-13). Rep from * 5 times more. yo. K2tog. Knit to end of row.

Knit 2 rows. Cast off knitwise (WS).

Sew buttons to correspond to buttonholes.

Every Day Cardigan

MATERIALS

RED HEART® Amore™: 7 (7, 7, 8, 8, 8) balls 6316 Chamomile Susan Bates® Knitting

Needles: 5mm [US 8] straight needles, and 5mm [US 8] 36" [90 cm] circular needle

Yarn needle.

GAUGE: 18 sts = 4" [10 cm]; 26 rows = 4" [10 cm] in Stockinette stitch (knit on right side, purl on wrong side). CHECK YOUR GAUGE. Use any size needles to obtain the gauge.

ABBREVIATIONS

K = knit;

k2tog = knit next 2 sts together;

p = purl;

st(s) = stitch(es);

* = repeat whatever follows the * as indicated.

Directions are for size Small; changes for sizes Medium, Large, 1X, 2X and 3X are in parentheses.

Cardigan is designed to be oversized.

Finished Bust (2 times Back Width): 50½ (52½, 54, 56, 58, 59½)" [128.5 (133.5, 137, 142, 147.5, 151) cm]

Finished Length: 28 (28½, 29, 29½, 30, 30½)" [71 (72.5, 73.5, 75, 76, 77.5) cm]

Notes

1. Cardigan is worked in 5 pieces: Back, left front, right front, and two sleeves.

2. Each piece is worked, back and forth in rows, beginning with a 2x2 Rib lower band. After the lower band is complete, the body of each piece is worked in Stockinette stitch (knit on right side, purl on wrong side). Finished pieces are seamed and front and neck edgings are worked in one piece directly onto the cardigan.

3. Back, fronts, and sleeves can be worked with straight needles or circular needle. If you choose to use circular needle, work back and forth in rows on circular needle as if working with straight needles.

4. Circular needle is used to work front and neck edging. Circular needle is used to accommodate large number of stitches, work back and forth in rows as if working with straight needles.

Special Stitches

M1 (make 1 knit) = Lift strand between needles to left-hand needle and knit strand through the back loop, twisting it to prevent a hole – 1 st increased.

ssk (slip, slip, knit) = Slip next 2 stitches, one at a time, as if to knit to right needle, insert point of left needle through front of stitches, knit these sts together through back loop – 1 st decreased.

Pattern Stitch

2x2 Rib (multiple of 4 sts + 2 additional sts)

Row 1 (right side): K2, *p2, k2; repeat from * across.

Row 2: Knit the knit sts, and purl the purl sts, as they appear.

Repeat Rows 1 and 2 for 2x2 Rib.

BACK

Cast on 114 (118, 122, 126, 130, 134) sts.

Lower Band

Work in 2x2 Rib until piece measures about 3" [7.5 cm] from beginning, ending with a wrong side row.

Body

Beginning with a right side (knit) row, work in Stockinette stitch (knit on right side, purl on wrong side) until piece measures about 20" [51 cm] from beginning, ending with a wrong side row.

Shape Armholes

Row 1 (right side): Bind off 6 (6, 7, 7, 8, 8) sts, knit to end of row—108 (112, 115, 119, 122, 126) sts.

Row 2: Bind off 6 (6, 7, 7, 8, 8) sts, purl to end of row—102 (106, 108, 112, 114, 118) sts.

Work even in Stockinette stitch until armholes measure about 8 (8½, 9, 9½, 10, 10½)" [20.5 (21.5, 23, 24, 25.5, 26.5) cm].

Bind off.

LEFT FRONT

Cast on 51 (55, 59, 63, 67, 71) sts.

Lower Band

Row 1 (right side): Work Row 1 of 2x2 Rib to last st, k1.

Row 2: Knit the knit sts, and purl the purl sts, as they appear.

Repeat Row 2 until piece measures about 3" [7.5 cm] from beginning, ending with a wrong side row.

Body

Beginning with a right side (knit) row, work in Stockinette stitch (knit on right side, purl on wrong side) until piece measures same as back to armholes, ending with a wrong side row.

Shape Armhole and Front Edge

Row 1 (right side): Bind off 6 (6, 7, 7, 8, 8) sts, knit to last 3 sts, k2tog, k1—44 (48, 51, 55, 58, 62) sts.

Continue Shaping Front Edge.

Beginning with a wrong side (purl) row, work in Stockinette stitch for 3 rows.

Decrease Row (right side): Knit to last 3 sts, k2tog, k1—43 (47, 50, 54, 57, 61) sts. Repeat last 4 rows for 8 (10, 12, 14, 14, 16) more times— 35 (37, 38, 40, 43, 45) sts.

Work even in Stockinette stitch until armhole measures same as back armhole.

Bind off.

RIGHT FRONT

Cast on 51 (55, 59, 63, 67, 71) sts.

Lower Band

Row 1 (right side): K1, work Row 1 of 2x2 Rib across.

Row 2: Knit the knit sts, and purl the purl sts, as they appear.

Repeat Row 2 until piece measures about 3" [7.5 cm] from beginning, ending with a wrong side row.

Body

Beginning with a right side (knit) row, work in Stockinette stitch (knit on right side, purl on wrong side) until piece measures same as back to armholes, ending with a right side row.

Shape Armhole

Row 1 (wrong side): Bind off 6 (6, 7, 7, 8, 8) sts, purl to end of row—45 (49, 52, 56, 59, 63) sts.

Shape Front Edge.

Decrease Row (right side): K1, ssk, knit to end of row—44 (48, 51, 55, 58, 62) sts.

Beginning with a wrong side (purl) row, work in Stockinette stitch for 3 rows. Repeat Decrease Row—43 (47, 50, 54, 57, 61) sts.

Repeat last 4 rows for 8 (10, 12, 14, 14, 16) more times—35 (37, 38, 40, 43, 45) sts.

Work even in Stockinette stitch until armhole measures same as back armhole.

Bind off.

SLEEVES (make 2)

Cast on 38 (38, 42, 42, 46, 46) sts.

Lower Band

Work in 2x2 Rib until piece measures about 3" [7.5 cm] from beginning, ending with a wrong side row.

Body

Sizes 1X-Large (2X-Large) Only: Work even in Stockinette stitch for 3 rows.

Increase Row (right side): K1, M1, knit to last 2 sts, M1, k1—44 (48) sts.

Repeat last 4 rows for 21 more times—86 (90) sts.

Sizes Small (Medium, Large, and 3X-Large) Only:

Work even in Stockinette stitch for 3 (3, 3, 1) row(s).

Increase Row (right side): K1, M1, knit to last 2 sts, M1, k1—40 (40,

44, 48) sts.

Repeat last 4 (4, 4, 2) rows for 9 (16, 16, 3) more times—58 (72, 76, 54) sts.

Work even in Stockinette stitch for 5 (5, 5, 3) rows.

Repeat Increase Row—60 (74, 78, 56) sts.

Repeat last 6 (6, 6, 4) rows for 6 (1, 1, 19) more times—72 (76, 80, 94) sts.

All Sizes:

Work even in Stockinette stitch until piece measures about 18" [45.5 cm] from beginning.

Bind off.

FINISHING

Sew shoulder seams.

Front and Back Neck Edging

With right side facing and circular needle, beginning at lower right front corner, pick up and k134 (136, 136, 138, 138, 140) sts evenly spaced along right front edge to shoulder, 34 sts along back neck, 134 (136, 136, 138, 138, 140) sts along left front edge to lower left front corner—302 (306, 306, 310, 310, 314) sts.

Work in 2x2 Rib for about 3½" [9 cm]. Bind off loosely in rib pattern.

Sew sleeves into armholes. Sew side and sleeve seams.

Weave in ends.

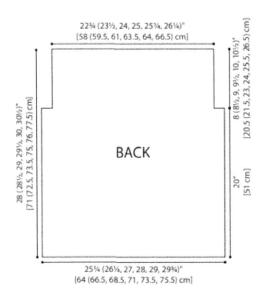

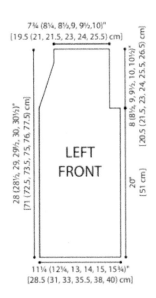

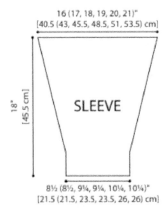

Chevron Trim Cardigan

MATERIALS

Caron® x Pantone™ Bamboo™ (3.5 oz/100 g; 180 yds/165 m)

Sizes XS/S M L XL 2/3XL 4/5XL

Version 1

Main Color (MC)

Ghost Gray (03037) 2 2 3 3 4 5 braids

Contrast A Indigo (03038) 1 1 2 2 3 4 braid(s)

Contrast Tropical Fruit (03045) 1 1 1 2 2 2 braid(s)

Version 2

Main Color (MC) Indigo (03038) 2 2 3 3 4 5 braids

Contrast A Ghost Gray (03037) 1 1 2 2 3 4 braid(s)

Contrast Tropical Fruit (03045) 1 1 1 2 2 2 braid(s)

Version 1

MC - 16-4703				

A - 16-4703				

B - 16-1620	C - 13-0935	D - 17-5335	E - 17-4041	F - 19-4028

Version 2

MC - 16-4703				

A - 16-4703				

B - 16-1620	C - 13-0935	D - 17-5335	E - 17-4041	F - 19-4028

Sizes U.S. 6 (4 mm) and U.S. 7 (4.5 mm) knitting needles.

Sizes U.S.6(4mm) and U.S. 7 (4.5 mm) circular knitting needles 29" [73.5 cm] long or size needed to obtain gauge.

Stitch markers.

6 buttons.

ABBREVIATIONS

Alt = Alternate(ing)

Beg = Begin(ning)

Cont = Continue(ity)

Dec = Decrease(ing)

Inc = Increase(ing)

K = Knit

K2tog = Knit next

2 stitches together

P = Purl

Pat = Pattern

Rem = Remain(ing)

Rep = Repeat

RS = Right side

Ssk = Slip next 2 stitches knitwise one at a time. Pass them back on to lefthand needle, then knit through back loops together

St(s) = Stitch(es)

WS = Wrong side

SIZES

To fit bust measurement

XS/S 28-34" [71-86.5 cm]

M 36-38" [91.5-96.5 cm]

L 40-42" [101.5-106.5 cm]

XL 44-46" [112-117 cm]

2/3XL 48-54" [122-137 cm]

4/5XL 56-62" [142-157.5 cm]

Finished bust

XS/S 36½" [92.5 cm]

M 42½" [108 cm]

L 44¾" [113.5 cm]

XL 50¾" [129 cm]

2/3XL 55½" [141 cm]

4/5XL 64" [162.5 cm]

GAUGE

20 sts and 26 rows = 4" [10 cm] with larger needles in stocking stitch.

INSTRUCTIONS

The instructions are written for smallest size. If changes are necessary for larger sizes the instructions will be written thus ( ). When only one number is given, it applies to all sizes.

Notes:

• Before working with Caron® x Pantone™ Bamboo™ multi-shade yarn braid, separate each color link and wind into 5 separate balls.

• Due to finite amount of yarn in each shade, pattern gauge must be matched to ensure successful results.

• Cardigan is worked in one piece to armholes.

• When working from charts, carry colors not in use loosely across WS of row, but never over more than 3 sts. When it must pass over more than 5 sts, weave it over and under color in use. The colors are never twisted around one another.

BODY

With smaller circular needle and A, cast on 182 (210-222-250-278-318) sts. Do not join.

Working back and forth across needle in rows, proceed as follows:

1st row: (RS). *K2. P2. Rep from * to last 2 sts. K2.

2nd row: *P2. K2. Rep from * to last 2 sts. P2.

Rep last 2 rows of (K2. P2) ribbing for 3" [7.5 cm], ending on a 2nd row.

Next row: (RS). Knit, inc 0 (2-2-4-0-2) sts evenly across. 182 (212-224-254-278-320) sts.

Change to larger circular needle. Beg on a purl row, work even in stocking st until work from beg measures 4" [10 cm], ending on a purl row.

Work Chart (see at end) in stocking st to end of chart, reading RS rows from right to left and WS rows from left to right, noting 6-st rep will be worked 30 (35-37-42-46-53) times. Break A, B, C, D, E, F.

With MC, cont even in stocking st until piece from beg measures 12"[30.5 cm], ending on a purl row.

Divide for Right Front: K46 (54-56-64-70-82). Turn. Leave rem sts on spare needle.

Shape armhole and neck: 1st row: (WS). Cast off 4 (6-6-6-10-14) sts. Purl to end of row. 42 (48-50-58-60-68) sts.

Sizes XL, 2/3XL and 4/5XL only:

Next row: (RS). Knit.

Next row: Cast off (6-10-14) sts. Purl to end of row. (52-50-54) sts.

All sizes: Next row: (RS). K1. ssk. Knit to last 3 sts. K2tog. K1.

Next row: Purl.

Rep last 2 rows 4 (5-6-6-8-10) times more. 32 (36-36-38-32-32)sts.

Cont in stocking st, dec 1 st at neck edge only on next and every following alt row to 18 (22-24-24-24-24) sts.

Cont even until armhole measures 7½ (8-8-8½-9-10)" [19 (20.5-20.5-22.5-23-25.5) cm], ending on a knit row.

Shape shoulder: Cast off 9 (11-12-12-12-12) sts at beg of next and following alt row.

Back: With RS facing and larger circular needle, join MC to next unworked st.

Shape armholes: Cast off 4 (6-6-6-10-14) sts. K86 (98-106-120-128-142). Turn. Leave rem sts on spare needle.

Next row: Cast off 4 (6-6-6-10-14) sts. Purl to end of row. 82 (92-100-114-118-128) sts.

Sizes XL, 2/3XL and 4/5XL only:

Next row: (RS). Cast off (6-10-14) sts. Knit to end of row.

Next row: Cast off (6-10-14) sts. Purl to end of row. (102-98-100)sts.

All sizes: Next row: (RS). K1. ssk. Knit to last 3 sts. K2tog. K1.

Next row: Purl.

Rep last 2 rows 4 (5-6-6-3-3) times more. 72 (80-86-88-90-92)sts.

Cont even until armholes measure same length as Right Front before shoulder shaping, ending on a purl row.

Shape shoulders: Cast off 9 (11-12-12-12-12) sts beg next 4 rows. Cast off rem 36 (36-38-40-42-44) sts.

Left Front: With RS facing and larger circular needle, join MC to next unworked st.

Shape armhole and neck:

Cast off 4 (6-6-6-10-14) sts. Knit to end of row. 42 (48-50-58-60-68) sts.

Sizes XL, 2/3XL and 4/5XL only:

Next row: (WS). Purl

Next row: Cast off (6-10-14) sts. Purl to end of row. (52-50-54) sts.

All sizes: 1st row: (WS). Purl.

2nd row: (RS). K1. ssk. Knit to last 3 sts. K2tog. K1.

3rd row: Purl.

Rep last 2 rows 4 (5-6-6-8-10) times more. 32 (36-36-38-32-32)sts. Cont in stocking st, dec 1 st at neck edge only on next and every following alt row to 18 (22-24-24-24-24) sts.

Cont even until armhole measures same length as Right Front before shoulder shaping, ending on a purl row.

Shape shoulder: Cast off 9 (11-12-12-12-12) sts at beg of next and following alt row.

SLEEVES

With smaller needles and A, cast on 50 (50-54-54-62-66) sts.

Work 2" [5 cm] in (K2. P2) ribbing as given for Body, ending on a RS row.

Next row: (WS). Purl, inc 0 (0-2-2-0-2) sts evenly across. 50 (50-56-56-52-68) sts.

Change to larger needles. Work Chart in stocking st to end of chart, noting 6-st rep will be worked 8 (8-9-9-10-11) times. Break A, B, C, D, E and F.

With MC, cont in stocking st, inc 1 st at each end of next and every 6th (4th-4th-4th-2nd-2nd) row 8 (11-10-11-7-7) times total. 66 (72-76-78-76-82) sts.

Sizes 2/3XL and 4/5XL only: Inc 1 st at each end of every following 4th row 7 times more. 90 (96) sts.

All sizes: 66 (72-76-78-90-96)sts. Cont even in stocking st until work from beg measures 12½" [32 cm], ending on a purl row.

Shape top: Cast off 4 (6-6-6-10-14) sts beg next 2 rows. 58 (60-64-66-70-68) sts.

1st row: (RS). K1. ssk. Knit to last 3 sts. K2tog. K1.

2nd row: Purl.

Rep last 2 rows to 26 (26-28-28-30-30) sts.

Cast off.

FINISHING

Pin garment pieces to measurements. Cover with a damp cloth, leaving cloth to dry. Sew shoulder seams.

Button and Buttonhole Band:

With A and smaller needles, cast on 7 sts.

1st row: (RS). K2. (P1. K1) twice. K1.

2nd row: K1. (P1. K1) 3 times.

Rep last 2 rows until Band, when slightly stretched, measures length to fit up Left Front, sewing in place as you knit, and changing colors to correspond to color change in Cardigan and matching Chart. Place markers on band for 6 buttons, having bottom button ½" [1.5 cm] above cast on edge, top button ½" [1.5 cm] below first front dec and rem 4 buttons spaced evenly between.

Cont in ribbing to fit up neck edge, across back neck edge and down opposite neck edge to first button marker.

Make buttonholes as follows:

1st row: (RS). Rib 3 sts. Cast off 2 sts. Rib 2 sts.

2nd row: Rib, casting on 2 sts over cast off sts.

Cont in ribbing to end of Right Front, being sure to change colors to correspond to color changes in Cardigan and matching Chart. Cast off in ribbing.

Sew Sleeve seams. Sew in Sleeves.

Sew buttons to correspond to buttonholes.

Knit Cardigan

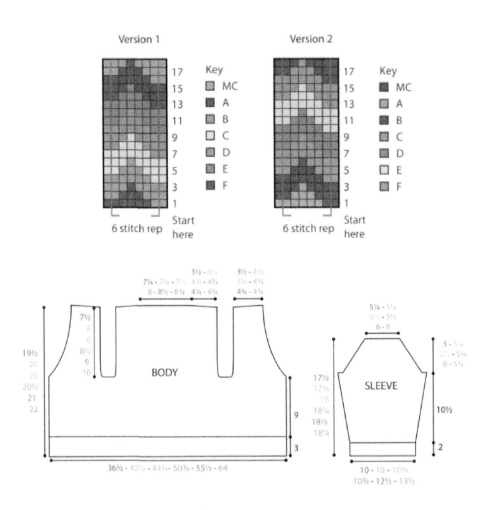

Printed in Great Britain
by Amazon

45160372R00056